JEREMY OVER

A Little Bit of Bread and No Cheese

D0815346

CARCANET

First published in Great Britain in 2001 by
Carcanet Press Limited
4th Floor, Conavon Court
12–16 Blackfriars Street
Manchester M3 5BQ

A CIP catalogue record for this book
is available from the British Library

ISBN 1 85754 527 3

The publisher acknowledges financial assistance
from the Arts Council of England

Set in Monotype Garamond by XL Publishing Services, Tiverton
Printed and bound in England by SRP Ltd, Exeter

For Marita

Acknowledgements

Grateful acknowledgements are made to the editors of the following publications in which some of these poems first appeared: *Critical Quarterly, The Frogmore Papers, New Poetries II, PN Review, The Rialto* and *Urthona.*

Many thanks also to Robert Feather, Cate Parish and Marita Over for all their help and encouragement.

Contents

The Poet Writes to His Family from New York

Well here I am, alleluia, alleluia – a hot pineapple on a sharp parasol!
The sea voyage was marvellous – six days of roses and cool hands.
On arriving in New York one feels a faint trace of the ink's
                                                    desperation
but what a sky I look for and am!

I am full of joy.
I live with drowned wasps and the legs of chauffeurs
in a drunks' lunch off Broadway, surrounded by canyons of lime,
where broken nightingales sing like bullfrogs in the Russian church.

My room is a capsule of air in saliva –
it is delightfully quiet.

Hippopotamus thighs and heron wrapped in rough canvas;
the meals here are a real challenge but I feel great.
I denounce everyone in feathers and plastic.

Last night I went to 'The Laminated Cat'.
The motley crowd of brightly-coloured sweaters,
tree trunks, clouds and turtles was resonant with
the delirium of astronomy and shepherd wrestling.

But no one can imagine the loneliness an unstrung violin feels here,
especially when the priest lifts the mule.
No one except Mr Eliot, perhaps, who, shuddering with rage, in
                                                    gold lamé
squeezes a lemon on the top floor.

The American people are truly as naïve and charming as children –
they all carry candles and wooden spoons and, this morning,
they began to take a sudden interest in folding screens.
Needless to say I broke into tears.
This is the subject of my first poem.

Next Sunday I plan to go to Coney Island
with some feeble-minded clergymen.
Like everything else here, it's a small,
small world with cloven feet in the pepper trees.

As you can see, I have begun to write in shoe stores
on stitched flesh at dawn. I lead a calm, quiet
sort of existence with white teeth in a box of twigs.
Such things are only sad from afar.

Yesterday I had a visit from little dead things dancing in the wind.
One of them made me a paper hat. I found it meaningless.

A pallid man asleep in a gardening glove is truly a child's dream
but when a thousand women sleep in a footprint in Peru
it is simply too much.

I may spend August in Canada.

And here's another strange thing — Walt Whitman,
with tiny red hands, bellowing at the roof's edge:
'LEAVE ME ALONE ALL OF YOU AND
I'LL LEAVE A PIECE OF CHEESE FOR YOUR DOG IN THE OFFICE'

Next time I write I will send you a copy of
The Slow Moustache (*Cow Slobber*) magazine,
which has published six photos of me covered with mushrooms —
I have a real following here.

I am going to Cuba for sure in March. Lorenzo has arranged all the
anthills.

Remember me to everyone
and tell Paco not to let the Pope dance too long on the dahlias.

Here We Are

Dancing down O'Connell Street: 1-2-3, 1-2-3, 1-2-3.
I look happy there – don't I?

A bit less clear now though – I think its Dun Laoghaire –
children perhaps, walking out towards cormorants,
or maybe just cormorants.

You can see the view from my bedroom window here – those are
tourists on the far side of the river, walking under blue and red
                                                    umbrellas
to give a sense of scale to the landscape.

This is St Kevin's stone prayer hut – that's his arm out of the window
holding a blackbird's nest all through the spring.

Here's Kathleen, a local girl, her face being
whipped with a handful of nettles.

This is a small clump of moss.
We stopped to stroke it for a while.

St Kevin and Kathleen again – here she is climbing up into his cave
and lying down naked beside him while he sleeps.

Another story about a goose
and an eel.

He's waking up now and pushing her out of the cave
into the lake where she drowns.
Yes, that's right – the same arm as before.

This is the deserted mining village:
smashed quartz and the smell of wild goat.

This is what a tin whistle sounds like in a graveyard –
and now, by a waterfall.

Here are some of the rumours of the lake –
we took an early evening stroll before they all got out of hand.

This is a question, after the rain,
by a clearing in the pine forest

and this is our uneasy laughter.

Love Poem 5 a.m.

The last grains of the night
sift through the branches above our heads
as we step, on bare feet
through the young larches.

We are too much in love to eat
except for the occasional blackberry,
which we nibble at
like out of luck foxes
on their way home in the morning.

We are too much in love to sleep
but, for the first time that I can remember,
I have just had a vivid waking dream,
of weary swallows resting on the ground
in small hollows – pockmarks on the grass body
of a golf course by the sea –
scars in the turf left behind
by golfers after their shots
especially their approach shots
to the green where the steeply descending
chopping motion
of
the club head
takes a rather large
divot
out of the ground
as backspin is imparted in order to stop the ball in as short a space
as possible.

This is sometimes tricky on seaside links, of course, where the often
sandy ground can drain quickly and become very firm, causing the ball
to travel a long way after the first bounce. In those sorts of conditions,
I always opt for the low chip and run approach myself: close the face
of a seven iron slightly and just sweep the ball off the turf like you
were clipping it off the dining room table. Better control and *no* divot.

That wouldn't leave anywhere for the swallows to rest though, I
suppose – no hollows for the swallows …

Absence

(after Neruda)

What's wrong with you, with us,
what's happening to us?
No! What's wrong with *you*, with *you*,
what's happening to you? I look at you
and I find nothing in you but two eyes,
two great dark eyes.

The rest of your body has disappeared.
Your knees, your breasts,
your waist
are missing.

Your mouth and your lips
have just flown away.

Your hair and your skin
do not exist.

Why, why, why
my love, why?

Where, my love, *where*?
I ask you, where is your hair?

And your delicate hands – your slender feet.
Ah! Your feet!

Take bread away from me, if you wish,
take air away, but
do not take from me your feet.

When I looked at the shape
of America on the map,
my love, it was your feet I saw.
When I could not remember who I was
I looked at your feet.

But you know that I love all of you,
your whole body,
those eyes of yours though –
I don't know – I do not dare,
I do not dare to write it,
those wild dark eyes,
those very big eyes were,
between you and me,
just a bit too big for your face.

Forgive me,
have I hurt you, my dear?
I do love your eyes, those sweet, most
capacious eyes.

There are rivers, there are countries
in your eyes,
my country is in your eyes.
I walk through them,
over hills,
next to the sea,
through villages,
across the road,
up the stairs,
walking, walking, walking.

Perhaps a day will come, small beloved,
when sleeping,
we shall walk through them together,
we shall walk all night long,
and at dawn,
we shall see each other once more,
face to face,
our love intact and new
and your feet,
refashioned,
together again.

Three Love Sonnets

'I made these sonnets out of wood … and that is how they should reach your ears.'
Pablo Neruda

1

I want to look back and see you in the branches
where, big enough for two, the moon lives
naked in the river on invisible wires
between your lips, a few blue flowers,

and somewhere else in my notebooks,
where your hands fly
through a thicket of confusion
to my hat,

like bees falling
through the pipes of your laughter,
down to the sea with its deep spoons

and the bitter footsteps of autumn
set loose under my tongue
where your feet are.

2

And when the earth is freshly washed, my love,
leave your lips half open, pale stones
for the gift of the rain.
The succulent book in the woods

is made of bread like the country boy
who, dampened by the sadness of roots,
drops down your cool stairway
in quiet sandals I had thought were lost

in the long-bearded silence of today, yesterday and
a quiet collocation of fingerprints as firm
as the praise enfolding the mud in your hair.

But I don't even know who it is you have squeezed
shut within the wings of each syllable of the January light.
Remind me. Who is it?

3

Your laugh, echoing at the rim of the wineglass,
it reminds me of ladders and stairs at the edge of the abyss,
the sad savage odour of the city's delirium, the dazzling
lurch of Diego Rivera whistling in the caravan.

Close all the doors of that guitar
before its petals wither wretched
as chairs on grief's vast porches.
Let's go down to the cellar, subject to spiders.

Love cannot always fly toward the water.
Bees hum, pots sing.
All the birds have settled down with the broom.

Your mother is still washing her clothes.
I see a future of joy in yellow oil and onions.
Let me rest there.

Ahead of his time, as usual, he smiled
on top of a hill, on a summer evening.
He was happy and the first to notice
that he was flying a kite.

Back at his house, on that horizon of emerald green ink,
the whole book of seaport colours lay open on his desk
beside slices of watermelon with a blue pitcher,
a sleeping gypsy, riverboats and pink paperflowers.

Later on, he liked to walk and talk barefoot on tamped earth
floors where too much bitterness would oblige us
to drink whiskey and get married.

'The truth is every sound,' he would always begin.
'I remember bells, the smell of cut lilies.
I remember an oblique stroking of the professor.
I remember you as a strange form of plaster monotony,
and, in another sense, I remember you, as a damp law clerk
howls inside a seashell, and breasts, yellow
as the yellow pigeon that is waiting on the far shore,
are sauntering all around.

But now the hoarse are sleeping with wheat
in a big barn and I feel your purple face
would be marvellous in a coffeepot.

Oh spoonful of mud, I am looking at pieces of timber,
for every thick and mournful movement of bees
leaves a confused traveller and something
of the life of the lamp in the window,
chiselled, like breathing, out of mother-grief.

After so many years,
after so many dreams,
where is the panther I am speaking of?

I look at trees and see violets.
I have to sell kitchenware
and I am sad.'

We applauded and raised our glasses as though he were still alive
with the kind of magic that finds, with growing astonishment,
a great eyelid in every stone;
an eagle amongst the rubble of the looting.

On other nights we probably looked at my uncles as much as his
                                                          poetry;
nobody would have given them a thought otherwise.

Stumbling on Melons

What wondrous life is this I lead!
Bees hum like well-fed bellboys
In their tidy rooms in the Campanula.

The black cat steps in the slippers of Ali Baba
Through a forest of asparagus ferns
Into a scented world of Mock Orange blossom,

Leaving no room here for the purposeful
Shiny green beetle and the clatter
Of pans, bill hooks and annual arrears

Of use and pleasure
Sage and thyme
The garage door

I have a penny in my pocket
And my eyes are blue
Discovery never stops
The goldfinch yapping

Yap yap
Yellow lorry

Yap yap
Red trapdoor

Ripe apples drop about my head
Cattle spread purple and green nouns across the lawn
And beneath it all

Beneath the luscious clusters of the vine
The nectarine and curious peach
Fuel

The hot neck of a sparrow in the hawthorn
The red patch left on your thigh as you uncross your legs
As Pants the Hart for Cooling Streams
And a plastic sandpit puts the pencil behind your ear.

Petit Pierre

Gradually, on all sides, everything begins to move again.
Sand shakes in the bottles and begins to sing;
soon nothing can be seen in isolation
and life itself appears as a mechanical cow.

Sand shakes in the bottles and begins to sing,
hens peck in the farmyard, imaginary hay is loaded, then unloaded
and life itself appears as a mechanical cow
turns slowly around a couple at the County Ball.

Hens peck in the farmyard, imaginary hay is loaded, then unloaded –
the next thing is this: a figure taller than the surrounding houses
turns slowly around. A couple at the County Ball
bid farewell to one another on a home-made zither –

the next thing is this: a figure taller than the surrounding houses
reads his newspaper whilst cyclists attempt to overtake a streetcar and
bid farewell to one another on a home-made zither.
A pig squeals in Butcher Nuttke's cellar and

reads his newspaper whilst cyclists attempt to overtake a streetcar and
soon nothing can be seen in isolation;
a pig squeals in Butcher Nuttke's cellar and
gradually, on all sides, everything begins to move again.

Divertimento

As a specimen of an accomplished starling, I may here introduce one visited by Mr SYME. 'We went one morning with a friend to see a collection of birds belonging to a gentleman in Antigua Street, Edinburgh and among these were some very fine starlings – one in particular, which I heard pronounce most distinctly the following: 'Come in, Sir, and take a seat – I see by your face that you are fond of the lasses – George, send for a coach and six for pretty Charlie – Be clever, George, I want it immediately'; and many other sentences to the same purport.

*

Everything we come to as we travel can give us help

*

If we could only listen to the rain – just listen:
up in the rain tree, the rain bird sits and sings
but the rain has forgotten how to fall
and all we can hear is a sheet of paper being
torn from the typewriter as a cow rips up
a dry tongue-full of grass from the ground.

*

rain tree *n.* a S. American tree of the Mimosa family, under which there is a constant rain of juice ejected by cicadas.
rain bird *n.* a bird, such as the green woodpecker and various kinds of cuckoo supposed to foretell rain.
rain *n.* water that falls from the clouds in drops; a shower; a fall of anything in the manner of rain – *v.t.* to pour or shower down from above, like rain from the clouds; – *v.i.* to fall in drops from the clouds, as water; to fall or drop, like rain.
raindrop *n.* a drop of rain.

*

On 26 November 1799 travelling to London over a vast expanse of Yorkshire moors, Coleridge gazed out of his carriage window and saw in the distance an immense flock of starlings sweep across the sky. 'The starlings,' he scribbled hurriedly into the skittering journal on his knee, 'drove along like …'

starlings *n.* proper term – a flock or murmuration of is like a fluid but coherent finger print pressed into the evening sky – black ink into blue. c.f. a chattering of choughs, an unkindness of ravens, a wisp of snipe or a superfluity of nuns.

'drove along like smoke … misty … without volition – now a circular area inclined in an arc – now a globe now … a complete orb into an ellipse … and still it expands and condenses …'

*

I remember all of this like it was yesterday
'But it was yesterday' says the snow
and it whirls around the room
like someone with a very big hand.

*

It's good to lose something you don't really need every now and then; an item of clothing, some hair, a tooth, a piece of one's mind. A tree,
of course, knows this.

Once we left the family Bible out on the lawn overnight
to soak up the late summer dew, and the next day
we kneaded the bloated black pulp and
put it in the oven to bake.

And when the door was opened …
a cinema of black birds.

More Birds

Two weeks after getting our Stannah stairlift it took me to Jupiter
webfooted
webfooted vermicelli
webfooted vermicelli booth

The Prophet teaches us to love God
caress
caress endearment
Is the answer yes?
I will not say
caress endearment
weasel flatterer
Is the answer no?
I will not say
caress fondle pet fawn
I will not say
I will not say

I have none other than this
the sense of coming to
of awakening
having a high forehead
to lick young fox

(a) clumsy slip of the pen
(an) eccentric halo
(a) shaky latin gun carriage
(the) classic tart
(some) hurling missionary your honour

We saw a horse
I asked him why he was here
I asked him 'Why are you here?'
He said 'The Prophet teaches us to love eggs,
eggs are from hatched chickens
water to thirst us quench our enables
do not pudding like plum Frenchmen
grow bushes blackberries on'

We saw a horse
He said that it was late
He said 'It is late
More birds die in winter than any other season
because they take up less room'

I have been in woods

                    on the outer   branches

  of trees

                                 in Autumn

          a few leaves

    so much

              can

be

                      a

                              few

          leaves

Lennart is inspired by the movement of trees
He said, 'There's always something interesting happening.'
His friend Raffiq is also a snake charmer
'Death,' he muttered, 'night, the sea, fear, loneliness –
more birds die in winter than any other season
because we can wipe our boots on them.'

'Oh Mum come quick,' cried Yvonne. 'Mr Baker, who lives down-
stairs, has taken his carthorse into the hallway.'
'Oh my dresser,' shouted Mrs Baker.
(Everything on the dresser goes SMASH then Mr Baker scrubs the
horses teeth, gives it bacon and tomatoes and walks it out again).

a coot in a willow tree
the artist's wife in an oak tree

an hour glass in one hand
a magpie in the other

the voice of the fool in the hydrangea –
'more birds die in winter than any other season
because they collect and hide the dust'

Alive at the bottom of the river belongs to chance that glassy cliff
feathered grasses   exultation   resonance   itself a kind of absolute
twilight dream of diving through dark waters in the wake of landscape-
closing night moon-illumined image on an unnoticed ledge   dim sky
over a dim illusion of lost wave-piercing pentecostal flurry high above
closing   as it is at our death conceal them so carefully we are not
born sense and by reason lighted spirit lighted is the flame   and from
this fact they are consecrated in their hour   the eternal hills as uncer-
tainty   prayers   flickers   sunlight upon corn-turbulent gulls intent
the air hungry mushrooms in a morning corner of shining webs
cohorts appeared suddenly   result   smooth   white   existence
nursery green   quaint   brought order resources sceptical of margin
babbling under trust   so made and become as it were

She leant forward in the lamplight
'More birds die in winter than any other season
because it's cheap'

Mr Baker took a goat to the public house. He blacked all its eyes and
eyelashes and put lipstick on its face. He stood it on the counter and
put a trilby hat on it.

Is the answer yes?
Is the answer no?
I will not say
I will not say
I said 'I will not say'

This is Just to Say

(after W.C. Williams)

I Hawthorn Eavesdrop
the poacher
thereupon whatnot inglenook
the idiot

art whistling
yo-yo whatnot probably
Saxon
fopdoodle bric a brac

forgive me
they were dentists
so Swedish
and so collectable

And Another Thing

I have earlobes

    just to say
  easels
the plug
the plunger

that whinger in
the *Iliad*

forgive me
          in as much
the iguana

    which
you were probably
shaving
for breakfast

       probably
scabby
forked bribery
for brickdust

forgive me
fortissimo
       demented
they were deluded
socialists
       swerving
and sockless
and so colossal

Mouthwash

Say a poplar	& mean	a deep sigh
" the forest	"	a drowning man
" a net	"	the lips of a sleeper
" a camel thief	"	a boiled egg
" up to the elbow	"	a goat
" salt	"	very well
" the crocodile has a lump on its snout	"	your Spanish aunt
" it is raining	"	silk or velvet
" fertile soil	"	there is a man waiting at the bottom of the stairs
" water	"	nothing in particular
" ice	"	nothing at all
" the sea is calm	"	she is tightlipped
" the well is frozen over	"	can you see her?
" a pear	"	a picklepot
" under a pear tree	"	a priest is coming
" gold	"	on weekdays
" it comes down the mountain flashing like fire	"	tomorrow
" bears	"	Vienna
" big ears	"	the earth is a beehive
" a beetle	"	the eyes of its mother
" she is fond of jelly	"	she is fond of dancing
" a green overcoat	"	a woman by candlelight
" a broken heart	"	a green overcoat
" winter	"	one who knows where the holes are deep
" spring	"	aaaaaaaaaaaarrrrgh
" a lizard on a cushion	"	a runaway monk
" a stone thrown at the right time	"	death
" milk	"	bring some
" your tongue	"	a fish two and a half times the size of this one
" your teeth	"	the moon is full
" the dogs bark	"	a feast of lanterns
" don't be frightened	"	I have seen the waterfalls at Penang
" he is getting old	"	where is his home?
" roll up, roll up	"	he can't hold out much longer
" he has fallen in	"	how disappointing

A Soft Tremulous Sound Everyday

(after Bonnefoy)

I am like the bread that you will wrinkle,
like the fire that you will iron,
like water purée,

like spume, or a comma, or the entire Christian church,
in a mural of light over the harbour,

like the bird of evening erasing the rivers,
like the wind of evening suddenly brushing past the fridge.

Imperfection is the Cemetery

(after Bonnefoy)

There was falsity, detritus and detritus and detritus –
there was also salami, but not at that price.

Ronny 'the face' climbed naked on to the marble,
a martyr to all forms of beauty.

Amy 'the perfection parcel' is soil now,
but last year sitting on Connie, death was just a secret pit in the floor.

Imperfection is the cemetery.

Autumn Arrangement

(after Trakl)

A monk, a pregnant woman in the stubblefield;
Evening inflicts convoluted wounds of bird flight
Upon the shattered grave of the grandchild.
Black mouths blossom softly into the night.

The sister appears in wild fruits from the dark bed;
Laughter, hideous and stark, drops from the naked willow.
Inside the tree folded upon God's living head,
The eagles shriek with the lechery of yellow.

An icy wind will rise within the greenish moonlit room
And angels step hyacinthine from the bell's last echo
To sink, in sorrowful splendour, in the church-darkened pond.
Bats seethe beneath benumbed branches in the crimson gloom.

In the ruined hallway midnight rains on the shadow of the father;
On the table a brown tree and two moons and a fountain and a gong.

Still Life with Fog Clearing

I don't know what you wanted with the fog anyway;
tonight you are clear and naked as the lightbulb that floats
above these slippery grass fields I row my boat across.

Inside the wardrobe light mounts up
then rolls out of the mirrored door,
like logs of silver birch down a waterfall.

I dreamt of swimming to the funeral on an August night, as you cut
                                                          the air
like the moon cuts the air, like another kind of music
that wants our bodies more than our clothes do.

The hole in her son's head is her open mouth
full of broken teeth, rusty doorhinges and screeching violins.
Tart green apples on a black plate.

I Sometimes Conceal my Tracks from all Humankind

1

I am a dark Welshman,
a joyous growth in the wood.
I irritate and frustrate the minds of men
as I sit here cunningly notched.

2

If I can
I step on my toes.
If not,
I hang on the wall.

3

Even a canny poet will be hard put to build a bower
in the pantry with plaited hair.
Let him who will, explain how on many occasions
the wind ruffles the waters with filigree work
and wafts sombre trappings beneath the girdle
mingled with honey in the thrashing loom.

4

I am by nature
a dull sort of sand
and in my womb
sharp chisels.

5

I often think of chairs
tenderly.
I bark like a dog.
It is very puzzling.

6

My stooping owner honks like a goose
right across the estuary.
My teeth are single
and celibate.

7

I was once a young woman
a glade in full bloom with rare ornaments.
Many was the morning I warped your words
into a history of marvels in threads of twisted gold
decorated with the aroma of spikenard.
Now I am found far and wide and when unstrung,
blemishes grips me russet plunder;
a splendid sight once I've
combined my mouth with a belt.

8

No one can find words
appropriate to describe my nephew.

of Mr Frampton, 'Feast of Roses', raised on dual-end support spandrels terminating in Agrimony, Bilberries and bleeding of the mouth, reputed to remove the freckles from the

12th Earl of Derby, 'Witness of a Ritual' and his Azure-Breasted congeners in ivory weave, their cartouche backs surmounted by Acanthus, Amaranthus and Dog Rose escutcheons throughout the Middle Ages, which, for a similar effect, can be strained through fine muslin after eating crabs with the intensely determined

Sir Charles Sedley, 'Slightly Scrolling Legs', and a pair of Cleavers to throw on the fire with the childish delight of

Lord Mexborough, 'She Will Rise Again', during the transition from the magical to the religious use of red tassels and the central lobed sconce, thought to make the heart merry and glad as

Mr Onslow, 'Food of Life' three seater settees, with squab elbows and cheerfully nodding Knapwort Red Muffs, once strewn in the Law Courts as protection from

Lord Lowthers 'Son of Exhortation' Brick-Red Shakebags, which attract bees with cabriole legs, often brought indoors, in the winter, by Victorians and positioned by them so that their long skirts would brush against the Pied Spangles of

Dick Gurney, the 'Small Stone' Norwich banker, a woman's best friend when woven into wreaths by the Dutch in the Middle Ages in the curious belief that

Professor Wilson, 'Lucky Spear' would carve Chinese cherry-wood as he descended in a parabola among the clergy, to give a more than usual mustiness to the

Marquess of Granby, 'I Disperse Wind', Lalique table lamps, and a matching 'arabs on horseback' teaset credited with life-giving forces often overlooked as snuff by three generations of the

Tipins, awl makers of Blosewich, 'Worthy of Desire' on a Padoukwood bench among the distant hills far beyond the unfulfilled promise of an explosion in the

Dean of York, 'Bent Nose', whose scurvy grass 'tree-of-life' Isphahan part-silk rugs were thought to boost the growth of nearby vegetables and discourage the hemispherical body of

Louis XV, '99 x 71 cms', a traditional finish to this huge race of warriors with a gadrooned wavy rim red lacquer four-fold screen?

Sgraffito

Neither swayed by hope of gain nor deterred by danger
the mourners have entered the tomb
and the promise of a new paradise
reaches nonchalantly into his waistcoat pocket
as a way of suggesting gentlemanly ease, elegance,
courtyard walls, and lightly touching hands in shades of grey
all seem to evoke and test the sharpness of the blade
and the gentle curve of Christ's body
describes a less ornamental world, a quiet screen
where the careful scraping away of the surface paint
as Adam scratches his forehead in bewilderment
to reveal the previously applied layer of blue
hills, a portable tabernacle, flanked by the lance and sponge,
and the flourishing cult of Agnes trampling
in the Netherlands before an apostle, perhaps, notes
the shooting star which is still clearly visible above
the forked beard of the hermit who hangs nearby
with a dish containing her eyes, two goldfinches
torn out of the vine leaves but miraculously restored to the
playful puttis with their swags of flowers and the midwives
in the foreground are particularly lively.

With Us it is in March and April

(advice from the Boy's Own Annual 1907)

Mr Reed has been dead for some years now.
Perhaps you had better try some other fad.
Opening the eyes under the water – not injurious, nor difficult,
                                    when you're used to it.
There is no such place as Chilli; it is Chile.

For Kibbroth-Hattavah 'The Graves of Lust' see Numbers XI 34.35.
Or 'How to send a boy to sea' – why not get that?
Think of the winter and what you are going to do 20 years hence.
You are tall and nature won't give it both ways.

It is a good plan to wet the calico and tack it down first.
The art world is very crowded.
It is the same in all flat countries.
Keep your money in your pocket.

You are nervous – you write as if you were a pigeon.
Put eucryl in your bath.
Put mercury in all the cells in which you have a zinc plate.
Try 'How to Shout' by E.J.D. Nesbitt.

The capture of Porto Bello by Admiral Vernon.
A very simple matter for a man with the right tools.
A bit of dry toast and a nice cup of Bovril.
The English leg is thick at the ankle and doesn't show at the calf.

We are of the same opinion as your father.
The belt is only used to keep the clothes from slipping off or flying
                                    about.
The Isle of Man.
Under the circumstances you had better get the machine you ask
                                    about.

Ask yourself just one question.
In the mean time squeeze them out.
The legs and arms.
The tent was not waterproofed.

Easy pillow, flat mattress.
A shilling a day and you have to wear uniform.
Put the bath inside the cage regularly.
Your mother and sisters will soon get to like it.

Good luck to you wherever you go.
Yes, flags and funnels.
Wind all in the same direction.
The ordinary postcard size would be best.

Daubed Loops

(variations on a sentence by Gerhard Richter)

In order to illustrate the fascination that jungle-like intertwining forms
have on me: as a child, after I had eaten all my food and while my
supper plate was slightly greasy, I daubed loops with my finger, curves
that constantly cut across each other and produced fantastic spatial
structures that changed according to the light, that could be reshaped
endlessly, according to the light, while the endlessly intertwining
forms constantly cut across each other, and spatial structures that had
eaten all my food to illustrate my plate, daubed loops in order that I,
as a child, jungle-like, and slightly greasy, changed to endlessly
fantastic and constantly daubed loops, that according to my food, was
in order on my supper plate, while spatial fascination with my finger
could be curves, could be curves reshaped endlessly, endlessly
produced and changed, as daubed loops changed the order, changed
the structures, the curves, the forms and fascination that changed each
other, while I changed, and my supper plate cut across the greasy
jungle to order daubed loops, could be loops, could be changed, as
my finger cut the light fantastic, and daubed intertwining, finger-like
loops, and a light supper that could be reshaped as a child, while I, as
a child, in order to illustrate that my finger could be food, could be
supper, had eaten all my finger, slightly cut, while I daubed loops, I
had eaten all my finger, and while my eaten finger could be changed,
could be slightly reshaped as a finger, I daubed loops with my other
finger, I changed finger and daubed loops endlessly, constantly, I
daubed loops, could be curves, could be loops, could be loops, I
daubed loops, could be loops, could be loops, could be loops, I daubed
loops …

For Instance

(from Hans Asperger's paper on autism in childhood)

For the item tree and bush, he just said,
'There is a difference.'

For fly and butterfly, he said,
'Because he has a different name;
Because the butterfly is snowed, snowed with snow.'

Asked about the colour, he said,
'Because he is red and blue.'

For the item wood and glass, he answered,
'Because the glass is more glassy
and the wood is more woody.'

For cow and calf, he replied,
'Lammer lammer lammer ...'

To the question 'Which is the bigger one?' he said
'The cow I would like to have the pen now.'

The Fur on a Dead Wet Rat

The fur on a dead wet rat
like the gills of a fried mushroom
has nothing to do with it

It's a Canada Goose
early spring morning
down by the lake
with Finn
the foot-brake
and a fresh wind in my white shirt
is a blackbird alighting
on the words cul-de-sac

spink

                              spink spink

        spink spink spink spink spink spink spink spink spink spink

The Irrational Element In Poetry

(after Wallace Stevens)

I

To begin with, I don't know. I don't know if I am competent to discuss this. I am afraid not. I don't know. Perhaps no one knows and if no one knows, perhaps it doesn't matter. It may be that someone else does know. I don't know. Does it matter? This is not the same thing as saying it does or that I do. On the one hand it does and on the other hand it doesn't. I don't know. But it really has, along with everything else, and for the most part no doubt always shall, in time, be something of that sort, for very little is ever not. I suppose I had very little in mind anyway. A kind of jotting. I should like to consider this by autumn.

II

Take, for instance, music on a winter night – harmonious and supreme and, for the same reason, happily oblivious to the broader definition of happy oblivion, and for the same reason. In short, a dish of melons.

III

Yet this is not, in short, even a dish.
In short, yet even this is not a dish.
Even this is not a dish, in short, yet melons.
This is not yet even short.
This is not even.
This is not melons, not a dish, not a yet.
This is not yet even a melon in shorts.

IV

Nor is it a book in an age as destructive as you please – do as you please and so on. It is not that nobody cares. I do not for a moment. Joy in time will be absorbed along with everyone else. Variety is paramount. Look at Madrid. And the old woman. So much depends on tight clothing.

V

Maniacs prompted by a circus? I need not answer that. A familiar glistening during the eleven o'clock mass? I need not answer that. But let me say 'herring' instead of 'hearing'. It matters immensely. The vast mass of clitter-clatter is still explicable in whatever form you like: a 17th century habit – that sort of thing – or a broader technique of effulgence usage.

VI

In the meantime we have to live with Miss Rootham's translations of 'A Duck In A Pond'.

A Poem is a Pheasant

It is not every day that the world arranges itself in a pheasant.

A pheasant should stimulate the sense of living and of being alive.

A pheasant is the gaiety of language.

A pheasant is a composite of the propositions about it.

A pheasant is not personal.

A pheasant is a means of redemption.

A pheasant is a café.

Money is a kind of pheasant.

Society is a sea.

The tongue is an eye.

Authors are actors, books are theatres, pheasants are pheasants.

Everything tends to become a pheasant; or moves in the direction
of pheasants.

Every pheasant is a pheasant within a pheasant: the pheasant of the
idea within the pheasant of the words.

There is nothing in life except what a pheasant thinks of it.

Pheasants take the place of thoughts.

We live in the mind of a pheasant.

Pheasants tend to collect in pools.

One reads poetry with one's pheasant.

All pheasants are experimental pheasants.

Pheasants must resist the intelligence almost successfully.

A pheasant need not have a meaning and, like most things in nature,
often does not have.

Every pheasant dies his own death.

The death of one pheasant is the death of all.

The loss of a pheasant creates confusion or dumbness.

The acquisition of a pheasant is fortuitous: a trouvaille.

A poem sometimes crowns the search for happiness. It is itself a
search for pheasants.

The Door is Closed, Double Locked and the Key is Thrown Away

In the middle of the snowladen forest, an orange grove

At the Banco di Napoli
Ginger headed children
Quirks for sale
Havana cigars at pleasing prices
Steady and decent and gentle
As an old lady's bunker technique

The gibbons love to sing on the eastern range
The equivalent of a high rise in music

But within the slippery deck of our resources
At the Banco di Napoli
A perjury couplet smoking molehills
Made Zoe hit the roof –
Shadoof –
Hit the roof repent and believe in the Gospel
Although his real love was for botany
Feet and foliage
Quiet hours
In a kind of wallpaper
Without all the bloodshed

And if any ask the reason
It is sexual
It is here
Staked out with abundance
In the sunlight on the window
It's a bit of slap and tickle
At the Banco di Napoli
With Tunnocks' Teacakes
Toomey Truck Rentals
Smash and grab the Tel Aviv canaries
And Tunnocks' Teacakes
At the Banco di Napoli

A little later
Spatula
Suzanne smiled to herself
As she recalled
Turning on the apricots
Lydia gave a short metallic yell
Almost without the full grasp of consciousness
And Zoe hit the roof
Repeatedly

Hat in Hand, Hat on Head

Bring me my sun hat.
Give me an orange.
Bring me a basket of oranges.
Bring the fingerbowls.

The bucket has fallen into the well again.
The paddy fields have been devoured by rats.
You are always blundering.

Fetch the broom and sweep the verandah.
These trousers are too wide.
Open the window.

I want blue cloth.
This is no good.

I want …
I want a secret world,
where immaculate white swans are floated on a tender mist.
I want the freshness of watered gardens;
soft light on a clean tablecloth and a pinch of salt and pepper.

Why does the mystery of shadows attract me so?
I love this room in the twilight;
music rising behind the low hills of my thoughts,
a sinuous nocturne for trumpet and gravel.
This is as delicate a business as digging
branch lightning out of a sand dune,
in a fish tank, in Basel, in 1921.
Such a quiet scene of towers and ladders climbing up
and away from our beautiful earth, and taking away
with them the need for thought as
a loose-limbed acrobat swings across
to the clockface and opens its plumed hat.

Reading now is wholly impractical.
Lunch corrodes in the porch.

Just a few words though from Jules Verne:
'Verily, happenstance, crescendo, yachting,' he proclaims,
slipping his hand inside his robe, as he picks
his way along the precipitous track.

'Strange seraphic portions of verve and comeliness –
I am abstract with memories.
The Roseate, the Sandwich and the Arctic Tern,
the …, the …, and the … fern,' explains Jules Verne.

'When our cat shakes her head, the sound of her ears whipping back
and forth is just like the whirring of a wren's wings inside a church,'
he adds, as he slithers down the grassy bank and a hundred windows
open on all sides of his head.

But this is merely secondary jungle.
Pound it in the mortar.

A steward in a frock coat
is a sure refuge from nature.

All doors looked alike to Dante,
for whom the end of springtime
signified nothing but stewed prunes,
apples, figs and plenty of it.

He sat in a forest reading, so absorbed
by the content of his book that
he had become each and every one
of the thousands of beech leaves that surrounded him.

Jules Verne sits down to join him but ends up on the beach
holding his wet sandals in his hands.
He crosses his legs and thinks of
Mata Hari on a bench in the park
with her hair in a hair-net
in a bag beside her.

'Mata Hari, Mata Hari, Mata Hari,
the world is full of demons
capricious yellow and bluish flames
in the depths of the night
for whom the end of springtime
signifies nothing but the domain
of uncontrolled proliferation;
of the chaotic and the eerie –
enormous wings – miraculous fish
at the edge of crepuscular woods –

Wait a minute – that horse's leg is in front of the leg standing in front
of the horse.

This is not a good arrangement.
Still, the room is beautiful and now the butterflies have begun
to sing in the seven sister ensemble where a hundred
hummingbirds cover my body with celestial roses.'

The point isn't to be blue, after all,
but to be blue in a certain way.

Serendipity brings its own reward
on top of one another in the Boardroom.

The Goddess Moira in the form of a tripod will now
push a herd of thoughts off the edge of the roof:

I love this room in the twilight.
I'll shove this broom in the skylight.
I'll 'ave this groom in the toilet.
Isle of misrule Inverkeithing.

Inverkeithing Inveraray
Inveraray Inverugie
Inveraray Inverugie Inveran

Insh
Huyton-cum-Roby.

He Fills His Pocket & His Hat Provides

And yet to squeeze this particular lemon dry
one must stop just sitting on a stool in the back yard
by a broken green fence, and seek perhaps
a woman arranging flowers by mouth
on a table smeared blue by the wounds of a butterfly's wings,
or a diamond of sunlight dreaming of a single bee in a field of
lavender,
or a cathedral sobbing on the side of the bed
its stained glass windows running all over the altar.

Yes, I know that I always say everything all at once
and then say it again,
and that sometimes I am asleep
in the middle of the night
when I pick up my banjo and forget
I am already smoking a pipe.

You're right –
I live in a perpetual state of metamorphosis
and my brother's cardigan,
but these few signs of life,
some cheese, a jug, a candle and book,
must be worth something surely,
although not enough, perhaps, to fall back on.

No, I believe in the end
one must fall back on oneself
time and time again,
and from greater heights.

When you've finished
close the lid behind you and smell the darkness.

Wunderkammern

1

'Sophia', the heavenly also
we may mention in particular
in tiers, like crinoline on
iceflows or swimming thro
Dürer's cornfield into and
out of the petrified paper
arrangement of things such as
the problem squaring the
concave mirror) divinity (as
though upon a mountain
described by Böhme as a
carapace of a huge lobster
divided into twelve plots
in Paris, where, already our
Evelyn's experience of mild
frottage has become ordinary
plumes outlined with a blue
that even licentiousness fails

2

ong. Elsewhere a mound in
a bower of convulvulus
involves sitting somewhere
and shaking and trembling to
the music of the swamp. Just
looking at a woman is a
'botany box' he claimed
simulating innocence, or
death, as well as other lines
most of them in his study
of rain or lapping waves
gladly. Another end to this
strap, tugging at an elastic
(voice: an explosive grunt
and a harp and a basket of
repetitions and displacements
which are identical in size
hats off with a snowball.

stone flowed like water
upon her boosome'. 30 Furt
be Magnolias? They were in
the hills to the north, a river
fluting the sound as though
there were no engravers. So
'Feast your eyes on me!'
The circle of lemon tree
mystics of the Middle Ages
rips: the waterfall arcade
lacked the stilt-like legs
of divers outlandish herbes
in a looping half circle
use of the word 'Thankful'.
It's not what you've got
It is the Parula Warbler
has reopened the door to
what they'd like to do next

4

'to choose to live in a cabin
to reveal the belching crate
is simply two halves of a
pane of glass, an open net
lined with sweet-smelling fir
pontoons on the Baltic, so
watch the blue herons pick
every corner and crevice of
'Our life is frittered away on
any whispers of yes behind
her. The wink in the lyrics
temptingly revealed? Was
rupt. Calling into question
the lines: 'Your solitude, sky
la mer at la pluie (Plate 77
I rejoice that there are owls
umping on a very large scale
and a cork 'bulletin board'

the lagoons of Tunis. Perhaps
and a sense of 'summerhouse
specimen of weaving and
at first glance, though, it
changed to a book) ... The
LOUNGE; IVY COVERED
AND romantic sunsets; chees
lined alcoves with dripping
reds of fish draws the ob
sufficient virginity of mind
in its 'pre-goldfinch' days
of Raphael's *Marriage of*
(New York and Mrs Morton
strangled in draperies.
caressed by plants. We
wooden doors of Maximillian
variety snails; cool storage of
no such thing as ugliness

6

and for pleasure in the fogs
in the woods, of the Ohio
Another woman is using a
duck; not nearly as strange
when under the influence
but Audubon's humming
attitudes upon the hemlock;
and a squirrel), inverts
Virginia. At most their
turning over the garden
gives room to the Beast,
the Creation, the *sex opera*
orangery for the display
of the brothers Gottfredi
snowflakes. This was most
95, 99), as well as evocations
of its own eyebrows. But no
more than a glimpse of th

So, could he have been right?
Did the well hold some strange, age-old secret?
Something to which only a few have ever been privy?
What had Mrs Maltwood uncovered?
Was there a long-forgotten quality within the landscape, known to
the Ancients?
Could it be that the Running Well was sacred to Odin?
Or had either Bazille-Corbin or Kingsford Harris invented the
Durden statement?
What obscure symbolism was this?
What if I were to use the ancient art of geomancy?
And who, indeed, was the nun?
Why were wrens put in the well?
Why not some other familiar bird like a blackbird, a starling or a
crow?
Or, perhaps something a little more exotic like a wood ibis?
Why doesn't a bird lose its balance and fall off the branch when it
goes to sleep?
And why do birds suddenly appear every time you are near?
Where was I?
What was that noise?
Whose house is this?
What did he say?
Who *was* he?
Were those *his* legs?
How accurate are the angles?
And who will carry the jam jar?
What exactly do you mean?
Does the anti-clockwise motion signify anything?
What about a doctor in your childhood?
What did a doctor represent?
And a house?
Chairs?
Would you say it was a happy childhood?
Haven't you said that you 'fortify yourself in solitude and love'?
No?
Someone else then?
That one over there in the corner?
With the pipe?
What about your time in Paris?

San Francisco?
Neither?
You do write though don't you?
Could you tell me something about the New York School?
Who is Dick's sister?
Who is Jane's cousin?
How many brothers has Jane?
Who is Jane?
And Dick?
Who sat in the very middle?
If all bloaters are herrings, are all herrings bloaters?
Have you ever tried any consciousness-expanding drugs?
What do Ptarmigans look like in January?
Could you explain the paradox concerning ambiguity and certitude
                                        in your work?
Can I carry the question further by asking you what your own
                                        answer to it would be?

Don't you know?
Do you know or don't you?
You *do* know, don't you?
Can I ask you what you are writing at the moment?
What ...... that?
Would you mind?
Hmm?
Could you be quiet please?
Is 'catching the frog' a symbol for fixing or understanding the
significance of the moment and 'only having enough material for a
hat' some kind of comment on your attitude towards the subject
matter of your poetry?
No?
Are you sure?
Who are you again?
What did she call you?
Ferdinand?
As in Da Vinci?
And you like bees?

In the Garden, In the Garden

'In the garden, in the garden, in the garden ...'
Van Morrison

If you are reading you cannot see and the other way around
as you glance up now from this garden to look out into another one.
You feel both elated and confused – wilder the farther
you go from the house and the sense of falling toward,
or ascending away from, yourself, as a gate swings open
onto the airy brightness of your own footsteps
so lacking in consistency or inevitability that
an echo here of reading the same page twice or losing your
place each reading the same page twice or losing your place
each two feet lower than the one below
makes the distant horizon delirious.

Has Ivanitza embroidered a skirt of many colours
her slender waist all askew?

There are many names for it
but I know what you mean.
And then, too soon, it was time for her to go.

At the end of the corridor a segment of blue sky appears
and suddenly he was standing up with his head
carried to dizzying new heights
and in marriage he did admire her zing
her lovely pigskin shoes and cries
'I want to live for ever and ever.'

Which is too bad.
I feel sorry for Dr Craven, the plants
and flowers and the animals and the birds.
'Do you think my father will like me
fighting the Ottoman?' he shouted.

'Oh to walk and work and use a spade like Mary.'

Hotel Hosenbugler

I

Can you imagine how many towels are washed every day in all the
hotels all over the world?
We don't need to know.

Nationally we tend to like our amateurs but this time there was only
La Vie de Bohème – splash – children filling the empty blue sky
                                        with brushstrokes
before someone turned the celebrated cellar dive
in verbal terms a cow
by Egypt – he'd never seen the pyramids
1981. Does he still feel that?

You start off in my head and end up in an armchair by a phone box
                                        waiting for
I'm not Joseph Wright of Derby and Hockney is

But it wasn't always so.
You experience the changes day by day possibly as attempts to cling
to a remembered world and India, in particular, or is this inhabiting
the modern world in a way that unquestionably does communicate an
innocence that rarely seems contrived?
It is.

But it wasn't always so
in Bradford and more recently in Bridlington
Utopias turn sour
Crumpets and Darjeeling
happen
We don't need to know how
the ceiling by Tiepolo is not entirely
a horse which has been flogged
but here goes.
For the moment he's not getting anywhere (And Bloomsbury
once unwrapped by the apricot light would not take kindly to our
egging the pudding but
we don't need to know how the apricot light (And Bloomsbury
can segue smoothly from the local economy to
you never know   listen   ears or   her hair

freshly crimped realises that only she can
but she is, as she explains, a woman cornered in a well
that gave you arms implausibly
strained through the prism of Mozart
90 ft up in an ancient ebony tree so that
closes Act One.

II

There was something quite romantic about that trip to Poland
It was springtime – everything was in bloom
the police and the various borough councils.

But whether it was flicking through the newspapers in the morning,
lazing through lunch, or simply enjoying a late night drink,
we were short of the mark.
Towels placed in the bath means 'That's enough'
Towels placed on the towel rail means 'Hello,
my name is Andrew. I have prepared your room
low over the gas fields of the Caspian Sea'.

Needless to say the yield is not great.
It was absolutely stunning.
We might as well have been reading out a shopping list.
Book of Lust
Deep Throat Island
Thrust Faults
Lucent Shields
Loosestrife
Haywire

Hello Andrew!
Hello green glass headquarters on the river!
Hello hope to have the pleasure in the not too distant future both
enjoyable and worthwhile in assisting you whether you are compiled
in an endeavour or in the space below so that I can trust you had
a pleasant pleasure and we hope to have taken the liberty and the
facilities should you wish to sample these during your stay whether
you are flicking through the newspapers, lazing through lunch, or
simply enjoying the trouser press
and Iiii eee Iiii eee Iiiiii wiiiiill alwaaaays loooove yooooou

But he is, as he explains, a long way off and fluttering
need not worry us as the canyon slowly, implausibly, through the
                                        prism of Mozart,
grew ears.

Needless to say, that's enough
Step out of line and there's blood all over the floor
but I would say that
rolling along, idly gazing out of the window at the next world.

The canyon is unendingly immediate
I'll use it again in just over an hour
Meantime I look forward to the opportunity for more
Darjeeling and Crumpets
peeps out from behind buck teeth:

'Hello, my name is Andrew
I have your complimentary Scotsman.
He says you're looking great
but he would say that
and equally if the winter is really harsh, the herders may need to eat
the goats before their coats are ready to moult.'

Journey out of Essex

Took a walk in the fields & spun up to the top like an air bubble
& O it is delicious when the day & as eager as a hope & bolted
through the hedge & gave a hearty shout & they instantly parted &
thanked God for his kindness & bulrushes & language & the envy
of his neighbours & sent some pootys & ferns to Henderson & he thought
to himself between the walls & the trees & on doing so I found it led to
London

& glad enough I was to find I could lye with my legs straight & mark
the crinkles of the stream below & the little dancing beetles thwarting
& exerting every inch & the hourly expectation & thus a man learns to
feel & encroach upon pleasures & the boat sprang upward & fled
into the next room & a company of grotesque resemblances & he gave
the Sea Ladies time & escaped a very heavy shower in the bargain

& the matter drop't & sniffs the frog & it was at last all to no purpose
& noise & men & hopelessness made me turn so feeble that I was
scarcely able to walk & holds no more her gown & the otter holes
& as light as eggshells & a boy coiled up asleep & more terrified & twitches
& bites her lip & the only thing he had left & broad old cesspools glittered
& shuffled along & noticed little or nothing & I was very often half asleep

& the nightingale keeps watering the currant trees & he owns one suit &
he leads a lonely life & so I said little about it & fell in with some
gypsies one of whom offered to assist & eat the quids when I had done
& Stilton for I was knocked up & was soon out of sight

& I was making for the beehive as fast as I could & I could not help
blessing the Queen & asked her a few questions which she answered
readily in a sort of trough & made a crackling noise like straw burning
& he felt sorry now & he felt exceedingly happy & as young as ever &
without end & the enlarged size & valleys of yellow ochre
& tethered ass & he said when you get through the gate you are

& what became of the boat & she said 'Yes it did' & made no reply & at
last burst unlooked for into the light & down went the scalding tea & she
paused & took up his pipe for another whiff & whoop & felt very much
refreshed & bye & bye on the Great York Road & hummed the air
of Highland Mary as I went on at length & everything was new & nothing
& everybody was for looking & he was all down to his shoes & teeth

& this is happiness – to lean on the rail & womanly excellence & samplers
with mottos for garden benches & on looking up for the sun & the
                                                        mansion worthy
& wasting away into everlasting decay to wander among the hills & other
matter & perhaps she was not far from right & so likely & they filled their
                                                                    hats
with eggs & lashed the pond & if you go with me I will show you the place
& this is happiness

& any place that giveth the weary rest is a blessing & as good luck would
have it it turned out to be so & so here I am an old wideawake hat homeless
at home & half gratified to feel that I can be happy anywhere & being weary
I crep't in & whistles like a cricket as he goes